HEN & GOD

HEN & GOD

POEMS

AMBER WEST

THE WORD WORKS
WASHINGTON, D.C.

THE WORD WORKS
P.O. Box 42164
Washington, D.C. 20015
editor@wordworksbooks.org

Cover art: Clovis Blackwell,
"Emanation: Hen & God," 2016, serigraph print.
Cover design: Susan Pearce Design
Author photograph: Rachael Shane Photography

LCCN: 2016962793
ISBN: 978-1-944585-10-5

ACKNOWLEDGMENTS:

Thanks to the editors and directors of the publications and productions in which these poems have appeared, often in different forms:

45 Mag: "Happy Hour"
Calyx: "Artifacts of Our Affection"
Enizagam: "He Visits"
Esque: "If you wake"
The Feminist Wire: "Fable of the Flying Fox"
Furies: A Poetry Anthology of Women Warriors (For Books' Sake Press): "El Suicidio de Dorothy Hale"
International Toy Theater Festival (presented by Great Small Works): "Tiffany," "Fable of the Flying Fox"
Ghetto Hors D'Oeuvres (presented by Brooklyn Gypsies): "A Dollar Store on Flatbush," "Black Friday," "Hawthorne Street, Brooklyn," "Misery Index"
Long River Review: "Toddler"
The Midwest Quarterly: "Second Date"
No, Dear: "Pittsburgh"
Opium: "Tell the truth, hen..."
Puppets & Poets (presented by Alphabet Arts): "Las Vegas's Defense," "Mandalay Bay"
Red Wheelbarrow: "Leaving Tijuana"
Rhizomes: Cultural Studies in Emerging Knowledge: "Black Friday"
Serious Daring (Oxford University Press): "Pirate's Admonition"
Southword: "Daughter Eraser"
UConn Magazine and the *Poetic Journeys* broadside series: "Mandalay Bay" (excerpt)
Umbrella Factory: "Amorette" (from Banana Slugs), "Misery Index"
Women Write Resistance: Poets Resist Gender Violence (Hyacinth Girl Press): "Daughter Eraser" (reprint)

Some of these poems have also appeared in the chapbook *Daughter Eraser* (Finishing Line Press).

CONTENTS

III

for Luke and his father

A whistling woman and a crowing hen
are neither fit for God nor men.

—*English Proverb*

POEM AS GOD

I am god and my cock
crows lightning
My nipples are thornless
roses, my armpits

a licorice forest
176 toes
my feet are pianos
every step I take is a song

I am god, I decided
women who starve themselves
will grow long soft fur
on their forearms

Men who sleep
with scores of girls
may enjoy their lives
but not their deaths

I piss liquid gold—hell, I shit
bricks of it—sure, I am god
but some afternoons
I lay in my hammock

turn off the magic, try to play
a fair game of cards, see if
I can survive by my wits—
good looks don't hurt

neither does a can
of pepper spray
I am god and my ears
are the wings of the world

I.

MISERY INDEX

We started measuring misery
in 1963. An economist traced its origins
to 1948. Our misery: 11.49.

A year later, we were far less miserable: 5.10.
Some experts credited the index for the improvement
much like those who weigh themselves regularly
inevitably shed weight. Though by 1951
it was clear this wasn't the case: 11.16.

We were least miserable in 1953: 2.97.
Almost everybody got a new refrigerator.

We won't forget 1980, our most miserable year.
June, in particular, the cancelled trips, too many
weddings, and Misery's 32nd birthday—
a crisis of confidence. Suddenly every baby
made her breasts ache, the threat
nearly invisible in ordinary ways.

Since then we've done our damnedest
to stay under 10.0 while everyday Jimmy
builds and builds. Each home sweet home
an apology we can't quite accept: the smell
of 20.76 on his neck, its taste on his lips.

FABLE OF THE FLYING FOX

He fancies himself   paedophagus pirate

    crack ornithologist   a seaman, really

navigating the tangled branches

        the wind in his nose
              carrying him along

    each unguarded nest
          a deserted isle aplenty

He tucks one egg
       between his cheek and gums
            like chew

careful not to break it
         onwards in search of

complementary flavors
       interspecial mingling for his mouth

Full in the hollowed shell of a nest
             he falls asleep
     paws and chin dripping

dreams his tail a sail
       catches a lunar wind

our galaxy

                          his interplanetary buffet

              Pluto   the bluebird

                flittering down his throat

Saturn's rings   silver feathers

        collaring the eagle's succulent breast

When he wakes

             to her talon

                    tickling his chin

mama unzips his fur like a coat

BASTARD BLUES

The baby inside me remembers you
on all fours, your wiry pony tail my rein.
The grown woman wishes it weren't true.

Daddy-gadoola mechicka boola bibbidi-bobbidi-boo
empty now like a corpse drained,
but the baby inside me remembers you

in graying jeans, biker boots, sleeved in tattoos,
the naked woman on your forearm, spiked heels, choke chain.
Mom growled herself ugly wishing it weren't true

every time you arrived unannounced, maybe you knew
I'd beg her to let you in. She'd crumple and blame
the baby inside me who remembered you

in an orange jumpsuit, how your laughter soothed:
Don't worry, it's like summer camp, behind the glass pane.
The grown woman wishes it weren't true

how much passes on, unspoken, what dreams exhume:
your father like your needle, his little girls, your veins,
this baby inside me remembering you,
grown women wishing it were not true.

PITTSBURGH

I was under the car
when she kicked every tire
said she was leaving

I thought she meant the mall—

I'da raised the bridges
burned a black fog

City that never—what's wrong
with sleep? Now that slippy
Jersey transplant dago chump's
got her locked in some high-rise

won't loan her the car
and she won't walk—tunnels fulla rats
and those shoes he lets her wear—

do ya blame her?

Maybe I shoulda known
the day she quit baking
said her new nails
might get swallowed
by the knead

Or if I'd fixed the faucet
washed the crud bowls
when she asked, told her I loved her
chipped ham on homemade bread

These hills are sinking, the paper streets
that made her calves so pretty crumble

Forty's mutt howls, the pipes
steam and clang: Pittsburgh's lost
its best girl. Pirates and riverhounds

what good are yinz now?

HAPPY HOUR

for Zev

The embalmer decays in his stool
It's not the kindest living
I buy his drink
we swallow thinks
and thank the glass for giving

Then he begins to sing
to pretty waitress Nancy
I pump their veins
with cellophane
he's howling like a banshee

The lights go up at two
I help him to a cab
he whispers *Jo*
next time I go
I'm coming back a crab
with a shell like bone, but red—
a bloody shell as thick
as the skin is thin
on a baby's chin—
a gull would rather eat a brick

PIRATE'S ADMONITION

Sand dollars and jellyfish corpses litter
her shores. The Pacific, she's an angry blue—
heed this warning: cross her and she'll swallow you.
She does not distinguish: pirates and surfers,
boys and girls, size is no lifeboat, my pearls.
You're the skin of a nut not worth her time to chew,
but if she's hungry she'll toss you in her stew.
You'll tumble in the eye of her salt seltzer
hurricane 'til you're coughed up like the whales
she leaves leathering in coves for—God knows—
the wind keeps no time, no secrets
as it tows death's rot-stink like a wrecked vessel.
So beware the poisonous white foam
snakes spilled on the sand each wave she breaks.

HE VISITS

From the bedroom, where they seem to stay
for days, she calls
Bring me some grapes for your daddy

I open the door, hand the bowl
across the naked man lying
under her outstretched arm

I remember a word
from Donahue, ask *How come*
you never got married?

You think we should be married?
he answers, gazing at her
smiling as she gulps

He kisses her left hand
holds it in the air
There. We're married. You happy?

I nod, watching my mother's eyes
narrow as she swallows
something, I think
the size of an apple

VEGAS BABY

The jellyfish don't fall like your cherries and triple BARS
rise but not like progressive payoffs in ticking gold lights
bend and stretch like the desert we've been told
surrounds us. They know there used to be more water
and though they miss the slow float across liquid skies
there seems now to be no danger,
this sea entirely their own. These jellyfish—

across the street from the Eiffel Tower, next door to old Picasso
unimpressed with the rollercoaster roaring past
the New York skyline—might know we think they look like guts.
They've seen this city gut our kind before.
This city isn't kind. Children burned in meth. Las Vegas,
your silver dollar electrocution, tentacles, cameras
and crank labs, your Liberace immigrant dream

Where's my rhinestone-plated Rolls?
Each rhinestone is a jellyfish. Each jellyfish a monkey
fur coat. Each monkey fur a shining Elvis
cocktail waitress who comes more often
if you tip that dollar no one else does. Let's dance
to the world's finest Prince tribute band. Eat deep-fried Twinkies
while Carmen Mirandas anoint us with Mardi Gras beads

How much to shoot my load in a whore's face?
What about that pearl necklace? Might I
gouge out her eyes and fuck the sockets?
I like dollar ninety-nine buffet breakfasts
drive-thru chapels, drive-thru lawyers. Sweet fat man,
your strip malls lullaby like swaddling blankets—
what's the harm in every last drop?

I will give you all my water for your bingo-stamper,
bowling sock, cigarette vending machines, trade your
tweaky stripper fuzzy navel circus spectacles
for one spin max bet straight sevens
one spin that sets off the alarms
sending Bugsy and the big goons
down to shake my hand

THE BOWL OF MILK

after Pierre Bonnard

Bend over, lady, hand it over, you're taking
too much time. Humming with your eyes closed,
thumb in my bowl while I'm here purring
like an asshole, thirsty as I'm alive. Cursing
tap water, fish niblets of death, your pretty
pink dress—I'll shred to ribbons!
Remember the velvet sofa? These curtains are next.
Give up those liquor pearls, my womb dream,
goddamn if you knew what I'd do for a lick.

NEWLY SINGLE

Sometimes endings are opportunities, she says. Her cheeks discredit her, rosed by early romance. I hear her screams when she's banging a new boyfriend, milking it like a tourist at 4 A.M. grinning and waving outside *The Today Show*.

Opportunity, sure, like when *The Voice* ends. If I pry myself off the couch fast enough, I can take out the trash, move the laundry to the dryer, grab another beer, and be back in time to spark one as *The Daily Show* begins. *Opportunity*. My mother's gastric bypass. Dry cleaners raking it in on hems and mends. Seven bucks for every crotch my frictive thighs burn through.

She was only talking about love. Trying to ease the blow. Some endings are not. A closed book is an excellent doorstop. Flat line. Smoking bag of stomped shit. I am the sinkhole. The last call ass grab. Scanning the room for a kindred pair of roaming eyes.

Six beers and two bowls later, we're talking on his mattress. A rare Sam Cooke album gets my shirt off. But as he furiously humps my leg I sober. Tire, dress, and go.

In fog-washed city air, the walk uphill is easy. At home emptying my pockets, I find the gift I forgot I'd been given, a dime bag full of the stranger's tiny laminated poems:

> *October 15*
> *I remember her*
> *in the ways the flower*
> *remembers the sun*
> *in the cold evening*

I know again. Knew already. Belch and sink into bed.

THE BUMP

Was there always this small hard bump between my shoulder blades?

I don't know what it is, but it doesn't hurt so it probably doesn't matter.

One day it begins to swell and soften.

After a while, I can't sleep on my back.

I try heat, ice and zit cream. Nothing works.

When it balloons to the size of a golf ball, I go to the doctor.

Unfortunately I cannot cut it out. The interior sac has burst. It must be drained.

He shoots me several times to numb the area.

The pierce of the needle is painful, but the tiny gurgling squirt

when the anesthetic releases is worse.

A sound inside of me that is no part of me.

I cry into the paper-lined pillow as he juices then dresses the wound.

A week later my mother, inch-by-inch

pulls the pus-sopped gauze like a tapeworm from my back.

DAUGHTER ERASER

He sweeps her rubber ashes
into the wooden pencil box
clasps the tiny silver lock
carries her with him
wherever he goes

Sometimes to pass the time
he opens the box and runs
one finger through the soft
pink shavings, piles her
like a tiny sand mountain
blows the peak softly: landslide

He traces a happy face
into her dust, closes and shakes
the box, wonders whether
to sprinkle her somewhere

Where would she rather be, really?
He does not know:
there must be nowhere
He never imagines

he does not know her well
He made her
He erased her
What more is there to know?

II.

Tell the truth, hen, let it out
Lay it. I can't lay it
Lay it, let me crack and fry—
I know it's in there, hen

don't try to hold it in
Take off your shoes, leave
your socks on. I'll strap
those shanks into the stirrups
Coax my meal out with an ax

I can no longer bear
your ballooning belly. Hen
I'll never use you—give me
your egg. I'll wash your feathers
Catch butterflies in the rain

to feed you one by one:
feed me, hen, release
your belly so big it's hard
to breathe, I'll bet—your baby
is my breakfast. Breathe, hen
I'll catch it. Let it fall

ZEBEDIAH LOYD SKILES WEST

18.
You carry our father's name
inside yours now

Locket, crutch,
or boulder?

Don't you remember the story of your birth?

10.
You begged mom to change it

Put it on your Christmas list, sick
of the kids asking why
your name was different
from your sister's

She bought how-to books
all the laws
said *We can't afford it*

Fresh off welfare, we could not afford
to make you ours

8.
After he'd left
for good, only
visiting occasionally
he came to your Little League game

That night you gave him
your baseball card—picture, you smiling at the plate
your name, batting average, The Braves

He scowled and gave it back
to you, back

Why West?

0.
Mom trying to push you past the failed IUD

Our father bicycling from the bar
to an ex-girlfriend's house
with me in his backpack, finally to the ER
where you'd already been removed

He saw you sleeping
nameplate matching
mom's hospital bracelet

Spat at the nurses, spat on the floor
you were a boy, his son
here to pass on his name

Screamed until the nurses
changed it to calm
the wild longhaired man
with alcohol on his breath
a toddler on his back
and some cut-up woman he wouldn't marry
too exhausted to defend her name

LIVING ROOM

When Mom tells me, *She wanted me to get rid of you*
Grandma drawls, *Now, I didn't...*

I stare at the squirrel
in the hallway tapestry
listening as they argue

When I touch its tail, the squirrel
like a word made flesh
climbs down the wall

and as it races to the rear of the house
I ask, but no one answers
Where are the dogs?

Barking. The squirrel tears back towards me
up my leg, burrowing inside my blue coat pocket
The dogs skid and barrel across the linoleum, teeth bared

Against me, the squirrel's heart
is a hummingbird's wing, a damp fever
as its piss soaks through, fear igniting

the dogs at my feet who jump, snarl, and snap
I try to swat them off, but they bite at my hands
and I yelp as one dog clenches hard on the squirrel

hanging by his jaws, jerking his neck
until the wet warms, thickens, and drips
puddles on the floor where the other dog licks

I surrender my coat and follow the dogs silently
dragging their kill to the living room
where still two women sit not facing

LEAVING TIJUANA

We wait with hundreds
of other tourists and shoppers
leaving Tijuana

ceramic Mexican dancing lady
and woven blankets in the backseat
a shiny white stiletto hidden in your boot

Behind us now the hills of shacks
crumbling in summer
like dead leaves beneath the feet
of stomping children in fall

We keep our windows rolled up
try to ignore the women
and ragged little girls
weaving through rows of cars
with plastic cups
or red flowers for sale
wilting in the heat

THE ONLY SON

Maybe I don't like church because nothing happens
when my brother knocks down the rainbow block kingdom
I build in Sunday school, a home for me
not Jesus, whose birthday makes people crazy.

Under the tree and shiny-wrapped it looks like so much,
but when we divvy and tear open the boxes, he always gets
more toys: a video game for every pleated jumper
and who the heck wants a HairDini?

Sweetheart, it's not about presents, the Sunday school teacher frowns,
scraping dog stuff from the sole of his shoe. I rinse the knife
to frost the walls of my gingerbread house. I've erected an extra-
       large chimney,
plenty of room. Gumdrop Santa, slide down. Bring me
       something good.

TIFFANY

When the fortune-teller told us our friendship was destiny
I already knew—like the sun always hangs at the beach.
Best friends since kindergarten. We've seen *Beaches*
like five times! We share hairspray and spray-tan
though she's olive-skinned
and it turns my mayonnaise legs orange.

"Don't you hate in the shower when your hair sheds
and gets caught in your crack?" I say
to make her laugh, "Time's up, I'm turning you loose, hair!
Sail to a beach down under. Tangle in a tumbleweed.
May the sun blond you always. Goodbye."

Summer weekdays I pretend I play piano,
the metronome keeps time. She cooks Top Ramen,
sprinkles in the sand-colored chicken powder
as I turn on *G.L.O.W.* We boo every Bad Girl
except Spanish Red, whose hair
is chocolate ribbons like Tiffany's.

When Sunshine moves to town, it's like everything changes.
Our new necklace: *Best Friends* carved on a heart
broken in three instead of two.
All the time, it's like a fight I'm losing.
Every day I'm turning uglier and fatter like my mother
who won't even go to the beach anymore.
The bigger I get, the more I lose.
I can't do hair like Sunshine does, can't share clothes.
I turn around and they're whispering.
If the sun weren't in my eyes, I'd swear one time
I saw her mouth the words—
but if she's your best friend, what am I?

Grandma says not to worry, time turns up new friends
like sand dollars at the beach. Besides,
she says, I'm lucky. My hair picks up the sun.

SECOND DATE

She fingers her amethyst
earring like an accomplice:
Yes, February baby
In a hillside cemetery

empty as a man listening
they sit back-to-back
blankets over laps
He's fiddling

again with the radio
tuned to the drive-in below
fuzzing during action scenes
She picks at the jellybeans

stuck in her teeth
Death is beneath us
she says, *and all these stars*
are dead so it's above us, too

A car's brake lights flash, flash:
Down there, look!
he says, *Bet they're*
makin' bacon

ARTIFACTS OF OUR AFFECTION

When I notice mold in my toothbrush mug
I remember the pigeons
roosting in the airshaft:
their toilet, their nest, our bedroom view
dusk and dawn

Monogamous, amorous, pigeons are known for their soft cooing calls

Once I had
three mugs, gold-trimmed
blond carousel ponies
painted on each side. A gift from your parents
our last Christmas. I thanked them
politely, might've even cooed

Slaughtered indiscriminately, the passenger pigeon
became extinct in 1914

One shattered in the sink
I sold another on the sidewalk. The last survives
demoted: bathroom workhorse

Servants and slaves often saw no other meat.
Pigeons in your dreams suggest

You left the photo I gave you
in the emptied dresser:
us against the wind on Golden Gate Bridge

you are taking blame for the actions of others, or may express
a desire to return home

but you took the bread maker
the banjo engraved with a golden eagle

Once used for carrying messages, pigeons represent
gossip or news. It is thought they may navigate by the sun

I take down the cloth paintings
we bought in India. Pigeon
this message to the moon:

There is no true scientific difference

in the afterglow shuffle
bedroom to kitchen

between a pigeon and

your Valentine bathrobe remains
useful—

a dove

releasing
each man it embraces

FOR SIX MONTHS

she's had a new lover
but you cannot
imagine it
cannot imagine
anyone naked in her bed
only your clothes strewn about her room
your hair speckling her sink
you know she's had someone else
but you cannot imagine him
he must not exist
or if he exists
he must not be as rich as you
or if he is as rich as you
he must not have earned it
if you cannot imagine her
with anyone but you
she must be
meant to be with you
he must not replace you
or if he replaces you
he must not be
as good as you
or if he is as good as you
she must not love him
or if she loves him
she must not

A DOLLAR STORE ON FLATBUSH

after Allen Ginsberg

What thoughts I have of you tonight, California, as I walk along moon slush streets with a heartache watching the hail pebble down.

Homesick and hungry for bargains, I went into the Dollar Store, dreaming of your geographic variations!

What umbrellas and what umbras! Brooklynites shopping at night! Aisles, confettied polychrome! Jamaicans in the paper towels, Dominicans in linens!–and you, Allen Ginsberg, what were you doing crouched between potato peelers and soap flowers?

I saw you, California, on Half Dome hand towels and palm-speckled pajamas, your mythology, reaching upwards like redwoods, offering the treasures of the top shelf to starry-eyed box boys and bootstrappers.

I heard you asking questions of each: Why's the spinach hella wilted? Where buy wine? Which way to the beach?

I wound in and out, following you and fatherless, followed in my imagination by my Uncle Ginsberg.

We strode down narrow corridors inhaling aftershave, lipsticking our wrists, our barks reaching like a hundred sunning seals over all the itsy-eastern states you'd swallow!

Where are we going, California? The doors close in an hour. Must I leave you?

(The moon is a moth, uncle; I touch your book and dream. Bend and kiss my forehead, the moon is in your mouth.)

California, you siren but I'm milked dry, skin flaking. I climb piano keys to uncharted planets, touch the scar ensnared by the rapture of your poppies, taste your whisky carrots when I corn-cream lightning. California, forgive me. You're five days away and uncle's getting sleepy.

How long will I stroll dreaming of lost gold past parked cabs home to my silent half-cottage?

Ah, dear uncle, salt-and-pepper beard, lovely old breath-stretcher, what California did you have when you landed like a gull on Lethe's smoking shore where Whitman and Lorca spit seeds into black waters that spit back?

THE NEIGHBOR'S BOY

I wake to Joe Junior crying and yelling.
Where is he? The sound is not above me. A cry
heaving with the growl of desperation. *Mommy!*

I peek through the curtains. He's standing
in the middle of the street screaming
Mommy! at the window above me. When our eyes catch

I snap the shade back, go about my morning.
By nine, boys know the rules on tears by heart.
What happened, Joe Junior?

Joe says *You better cool it before you get to school*
or everybody's gonna laugh at you.
Last night while I tried to write, I listened

to them creak, pump, and grunt. They're
both big people, Joe especially—some things
can't be done quietly. What did it sound like

from inside, Joe Junior—what I heard
but louder, awash in cartoons from the TV you cranked
lying on your stomach close to the screen to make it

as much as you could all you could hear?
Bastards beget bastards.
Believe it, Joe Junior. One bastard to another.

Believe me as your mother
lights a cigarette and walks you to the bus stop
for the first time this year.

24-HOUR ALL-YOU-CAN-EAT BUFFET!

Big Burt. Big Burt.
They call him a teddy bear,
well, that's just politeties.
He's one double jumbo
extra-large (triple
after the holidays)
scarecrow with newspaper brains.

He defends the sacred saltlick,
salivates at the henhouse door.
Yes, he likes to eat. Gruff gruff.
Sure, he likes to eat. Gruff gruff.
Everybody's got something
they like to do too much.

She shippy-shops. He shoots up.
Burt gruff gruffs.
And somebody prays for us all.

LAS VEGAS'S DEFENSE

So I like to drink. Who doesn't? So I don't like
drinking alone. Who does? Thirsty? I'm goddamn
dehydrated. It's called desert. Guy's bound to get lonely.

I was a beautiful baby, stopped the Mormons dead in their tracks.
Didn't take 'em long to empty my subterranean springs.
So I'll trade you for it, baby: my sweet surge, your slow electrocution.

Call me seducer. Hypnotist, swindler, hornswaggler,
drug peddler, bamboozler, back breaker, addict maker.
Call me a blight: what's wrong with America. Cheat,
double crosser, inheritance wrangler, blood letter,
bank drainer. Fat man with no green belt?
Hell, I've never owned a belt. How else could I have spread
across this desert, melted all that cactus? Call me
what you like. They'll still come. Now you listen to me.

Bring your Great Lakes. Bring your Dead Sea.
Some salty Pacific, please. Take my rhinestone bootstrap dream.
Come inside, where the air's conditioned.
Don't stand out there in the heat.
I'll comp you a drink if you give me what I need.
Dam it to me. Pipe it to me. Feed me. Baby's thirsty.
Just a suckle. Just a taste. My teats ran dry.
Does that mean I don't deserve to grow?
Do I deserve to die?

Call me what you like. The old folks call me love, call me
sunshine blanket. Heaven sent, or even heaven.
They're almost there. Where can a guy get a drink around here?

Feeding them all-you-can-eat. Who turns the other cheek
while your grandma sneaks napkin-wrapped leftovers

into her purse? Who's taking care of her?
Me and that yappy spoiled little dog, that's who
calls me home, resting place, permanent vacation.
Who wipes the toilet water from granddad's saggy nuts?
One of mine do. And she can own herself
a condo here for doing it, too.

So if you call me thief, call me Nurse Thief.
Bed sore mender, wrinkled ass wiper. He calls me
thank-god-I-don't-know-where-I'd-be-without-you. The woman
wheeling him into the casino calls me possibility...

III.

MANDALAY BAY

The jellyfish aren't really purple
the voice in the wand explains:

without the black light
the smuck is invisible

A smuck, it calls them, or a bloom
like a pack of dogs

Tapping the columnar tank, a kid says
they look like guts

if guts grew wings
but I know they're endless drifters

They'd have never flown
to Las Vegas

IF YOU WAKE

monkey in your bed
quarter on your tongue
sugar rotted veins
crumbled castle lungs
on cliffs you did not climb
in coves no man can touch
each word an unsolved crime
choking on the thrush

if the bud blooms ash
if you catch a growl
diamonds curse the coal
every star browns out
buses drown in leaves
buildings shed their skins

if it's March and gutted
swine hang on roadside limbs

BLACK FRIDAY

for Jdimytai Damour, 1974-2008

The hand scrawled sign on the glass door says

Blitz Line Starts Here!

Marching through   Get out of the way   Trampolining
pulse pulse crowd   Are you on line?   Were we ever?
Black Friday   what have we done?   Made hungry

we became—

        bombarded with orders to buy, sir, were we not?

an it   a surge   some tornado

                                          deciding

                                    its own direction

Midnight wolves   hounds and hunters

                rattle the walls!   Torch, lynch, and jeer!

      Tell them we were a meteor
      with no more determination
      stepping backwards off the canyon ledge
      thousands of years in the future
      whispering wherever we go from here
      we go   hurled   at the mercy of   unwillingly
      here   for   ourselves   falling

without sweetness

the neighbor's boy fishing the old dog from the pool

the freezing smoking ice

we were not anything   more material
than half willing   half hateful

          whispering wherever we go from here we go hurled
          so willingly—
          here for ourselves

Stompers and stumblers   moving with the avalanche   the motion
of falling forward   becoming the mouth to avoid being eaten
Swim with the wave   Don't turn to face it   and if someone's leash
gets caught on a rock   What held us down was us and each of us
kicking our own way out felt the hand on our foot
only later we admit was his

Blitz Line Starts Here!

The thousands of pounds careening into you
was people, not metal, not the struck girl's
two hundred foot flight, but both of you
landed, later someone rolled
both of you over

nothing could be
everything's been done

Blitz Line Starts Here!

Reports   6′5   270   by sheer size qualified

like a football player   Welcome to Wal-Mart   man the door guard the line   not the usual type   not a regular day

Welcome to Wal-Mart   the old white greeter   too broke to retire

Welcome to Wal-Mart   guard the door   man the line

Black Friday   contract labor   needed that day

     big day, big man   only today   pat on the back

        more bull   to keep us cows   in line

      us herd   crowding   the narrow chute

Our sales news is overshadowed by the tragic incident
at our Valley Stream store
We consider Mr. Jdimytai Damour
part of the extended Wal-Mart family
and are saddened by his death

Your father tells reporters you were a good son
Your mother, home in Haiti, came as soon as she heard

Jdimytai, they said
hardworking, a good son, loved movies and anime
wrote poetry

    Temporary employee
              post-mortem promotion
                       an extended member
                       of the family

No benefits
but that's no different, no union, no
surprise, no one noticed
someone take
the hinges off the doors

no one said
if they did, anyway

Blitz Line Starts Here!

so what / we say / who pushed / we pushed / who of we
pushed / us pushed / we pushed forced forward / moving
with / what wouldn't stop coming / blanketing all in its way /
bending metal / bowing metal / out of the way / shattering
glass / not without / precision / removing hinges / try to swim
to / the waterfall / won't let you / the shy that acts brash /
smacks your wrist / snaps back / we say it was not us / who,
then? / don't get fresh now / please exit the store / we don't
answer / a man has died / we stood outside all night / they
told us to come / buy / what's this got to do with us / here
now / they say we cannot buy / leave everything behind / go
back outside / he isn't family / he was / not buying / won't
bring him back / in the face of great misfortune / we've been
instructed to buy / solutions / the nation's way / mourn / we
celebrate / breathing / nothing is optional / eat / we have no
choice / we are just / hosts / starving / we are / our worms /
demanding / eating / we / always starving / Jdimytai / don't
keep us from our food / we beg / Jdimytai / they won't listen /
feed us / Jdimytai / we froth / we fed / we'll feed on you

Blitz Line Starts Here!

It's the most wonderful time —

Out of the red, into
our one good black, though no less sinister
than our black plague, blackmail, some fever, black
balling, some disease, explain away somehow
this mercilessness: some other country, maybe?
Bloodline craving, want masked as need, need
and out drops the bottom, no
money, never no credit, no, Christmas
is never cancelled, we need, we need, we'll stand
all night laughing in front of Wal-Mart, huddled
for warmth, someone selling hot dogs,
hot chocolate, but when the sun comes up
or maybe just before, as 5 A.M. ticks closer
something changes, we who've known
and never known hunger
call it that, pressing close to one another
up against the doors, the weight of we
heaving, shattering glass, trampling a man to—

Blitz Line Starts Here!

Jdimytai Damour

EL SUICIDIO DE DOROTHY HALE

after Frida Kahlo

angel-armed clouds
cannot catch what falls
from the 33rd floor: you

who leapt, the wind flips
head first, diving, we wish
asphalt was water
but blood pools the frame
above which you lie
twenty rosebuds pinned to your black velvet gown

your nude-stockinged foot hangs
over the inscription, pointing
to your name: Dorothy, who stares
us down, Dorothy
holds out her hand, Dorothy
we see you fall

who saw you land

BANANA SLUGS

for Sarah Ann Mercer

I.

You who hate poetry, you who
secretly read mine, admit it a month later
You who eat bowls of dry oatmeal sprinkled with brown sugar
whose first batch of cookies poisons me, throw up
in the dining hall, on the track, at the taqueria
You who hide in the bathroom in the vintage chiffon dress
prefer khaki shorts, Birkenstocks, blue scarf headbands
You who lie on the dorm room floor reading *Runner's World*,
The Second Sex, *Vogue*, *The Voyage Out*
You who drown in my jeans, despise your upper arms
lock yourself on the balcony to sunbathe nude
You spray on tan, run past us in a beige sports bra
You who won't return my green sweatshirt
You, I thought I knew you
You, I cannot judge
won't turn off *Automatic for the People*
won't let me put our names on the answering machine
You who buy our groceries, offer to buy my books
plan how we'll study for the GRE
ask me to sneak a pound of grapes into the movie
You who want to take us all along to France
You who try so hard to get me to talk
make 2 A.M. crank calls 'til we're giggling like fifth graders
stop a stranger on the street to ask about her running shoes
You can't bowl so I take your turn
can't skate, make me hold your hand
can't find your ID card, "Leave it unlocked, lost my key
again" "Under the papers on your desk, like always"
You who say you'll never have children or marry
in every mirror bring your face to a point like Mrs. Dalloway
You ate three peaches three nights ago

You go running every day
You come home
knee brace, plastic poncho, running through the rain
smelling like a dog after running in the rain
You who always come home on time

II.

Two policemen come to our room.

     She darted out into the road.

          Maybe on purpose,

             do you know—

             had some reason to—

      No, I know—

The woman flew, then skidded
118 feet from the point of impact
before she came to rest.

          Amorette,

the driver, was uninjured.

      Amorette, does that mean
              little love?

    We thought she was chased,
          a man, a mountain lion—

           No. This
           is where
           she landed.

Amorette does that—

                              Mean little love.

A motorcyclist rolled her over,
tried CPR—

                              It might be best for you to
                              tell her mother.

                                        Amorette,

          does that mean
          little, love?

III.

strike of a car
blow to the head
one hundred eighteen foot flight

orange oval
in the weeds to the left
where a size 8½ running shoe landed

crash fire-fire bomb-fire crash-lion pounce-door
closed on me in a closet full of fire

orange oval
in the dirt and gravel to the right
where the other shoe landed

hollow echo
oven door closed
late May morning, last warm sleep

crash fire-fire bomb-fire crash-lion pounce-door
closed on her in a closet full of fire

blood shadow
on the asphalt
still, six months later

IV.

On the sidewalk
a bird lies, dead
eyes open
blood trickles
from its beak

How much more poured from her mouth

and years after she's gone

why am I asking?

V.

In the redwood forest
on the trail to the library
the first week of school
I didn't see it until you said
You stepped on it!

No banana, no sun
ripe lemon is so yellow

Squashing our mascot
seemed a bad omen
but you said not to worry

    o

How it felt under my foot
I've forgotten, but not
your hair, dyed
Marilyn-white, your legs
bolts of lightning, turquoise
running shorts, deer grazing
at our bedroom window

    o

I left it on the path

Never lurked past its home
like a driver
dumbed by guilt

Was it hauled off
by beetles, devoured under a fern?

o

They think she's up there somewhere
sitting on a cloud, your mother says
when I show her the plastic crystal
angels your stepfamily gave out
at your on-campus memorial

I visit her whenever
I can, you boxed in oak
on her bookshelf in good sunlight
facing the Oregon pines

o

Dreaming, I'm a redwood
tearing myself up at the roots
to crush her, make her pay

attention. Dreaming
wind, I gust you
from her swerving path, dreaming

I'm the driver, somehow I,
the one asked to tell your mother—

o

I try to believe your dust
has promise, impatient
for some return

VI.

She did not bury you. You did not want to be buried. She builds
a barn, a gazebo, a riding arena. Asks me to help her plant daffodils.
Distractions are not replacements, she says, *but now I understand
little old ladies with dogs they treat like babies.*

We dig the ground along the fence line just deep enough.
Cover the bulbs gently.

What metaphor will comfort us? What birth from this burial?
Daffodils banana yellow. Beautiful
grow. Countless

TODDLER

She bats at the overgrown grass
all around her, the wind plays
eucalyptus maracas. Leaves break,
flutter, and drift like kites let go

She grabs a weed taller than she is
with both hands, leans away
with all her weight until it breaks,
rocking her back, forward

A family of snails
fascinates her, their familiar crawl,
glittering slime trails, squishy bodies,
shells as delicately stiff as the paint
she chips off the kitchen wall,
strapped in a high chair
waiting to be fed

She puts two in her mouth,
coos to herself, feeling
them move across her tongue
as if she had three tongues
or food could eat her

When she laughs
one falls out, lands
shell-down in the mud

She turns him over. They each
inch on, unfazed

HAWTHORNE STREET, BROOKLYN

My nap ends with a knock
Three boys from the block
asking to borrow the red pedal truck
thick with dust on my porch
since the neighbors moved out

The boys on my block
stalking the rat
that chases the squirrel
past double-dutch girls
who sneer but don't stop

Each stoop is a yard
the sidewalk, a park
Two climb in, one pushes
Thank you, miss!
Have it back by dark

Three boys speed the block
the sun is their clock

BOMBAY LOVE

After years, I google you, a man
with your name is dead. Bombay renamed
the year we fell in love, you said *You can
call me Harry*. Though as strangers craned

to photograph me in hewn mountain caves
I wondered. Your mother's soft dismay
All the gulab jamun she ate. I crave
your sinews' pleas at times, sugar always,

nights my tales gripped you, my fingers, your hair.
2,555 days
I was your red paper kite. When tired
you released me. I ignited, ablaze

in true flight. Still, Sheheryar, I think sometimes
you are with me like this dead man. Hear this, Mumbai.

PRACTICE

Kimberly twists her cleat into the dirt
Monet holds my arm, hopping up and down in place

Karina asks a question about the field's dimensions
as Joi floats a beauty
into the top right corner

Babbette sprints away
to recover Heidi's misfire

Hazel touches her shoulder, whispers
It's OK, sister

Christina slumps in the bleachers
waiting for me to see
why she doesn't want to play

Terry cries again, somebody called her a baby
Maybe Emiah, staring upwards, her thumb in her mouth

Benette softens the blow with dandelions
Rachel chains together, making bracelets

When a man walking a dog asks
How many are yours?
everybody laughs

except Wendy
eyes narrowed, arms wide
guarding the goal like a mother
would her child

POME

Yes, she is

my pome

but she's no false fruit

We resent the implications

She is more than her ovaries

She would like you to listen

but knows you prefer she listen

She listens to love

and loves to listen

the thunder as a toddler tears

across a hardwood floor

Hostess, always gracious

invites everyone in

for bone marrow

pound cake

lights pencil tips on fire

to soften the lead

divines the buffalos' escape

in a strand of mermaid hair

In his poem's

          thistle

              cicada

my pome sees

the slum

the people she knows who stay there

how she wishes they could leave

My pome is abandoned

been abandoned

countless times

Wait,

        I mean

she's shameless

watch her

cum-crusted

asshole

If my pome was President

she'd redistribute the nation's wealth,

free Mumia, abolish prisons,

universalize public health

Alas she's just a tattoo artist

with a mostly steady hand

She's blessed with x-ray vision

and she's checking out your yams

Grandma kneels on the back steps

to cut grandad's toenails

My pome, the toenails, and the dirt

beneath the pomegranate tree

the clawfoot bathtub by the broken fence

where the squirrels swim at night

trash from the trailer

landed on the beach

where schoolchildren

harvest seashells

Pome collects the most

to impress her teacher

classmates gather before her

she gives each

a new name

ropes seagulls with kelp lassos

until a grown-up screams *Stop!*

races the crest

of each wave to the shore

My pome cleans the house

with the music loud

singing off key

I'm gonna live forever

she is the crackle and breath

at the end of every record

NOTES

Several poems include found language from the following sources:

Artifacts of Our Affection
    "Passenger Pigeon" entry on reference.com.
    "Pigeon" entries on dreammoods.com and in
        Encyclopedia section on infoplease.com.
    "Pigeons and Doves" entry in Rainforest Bird Index on
    rainforest-australia.com.

Banana Slugs
    "Nightswimming," a song written by Mike Mills and
    released by R.E.M. in 1993.
    "Jogger Killed Crossing Empire Grade Road," *Santa
    Cruz Sentinel*, May 25, 1997.

Bastard Blues
    Variation on a line from "Bibbidi-Bobbidi-Boo," a song
    written in 1949 by Al Hoffman, Mack David,
    and Jerry Livingston and popularized in the 1950
    Disney film, *Cinderella*.

Black Friday
    "Wal-Mart Employee Trampled to Death," *New York
    Times*, November 28, 2008.
    "Wal-Mart Reports November Sales," December 4, 2008,
        press release, Wal-Mart News Archive.
    "It's the Most Wonderful Time of the Year," a song
    written in 1963 by Edward Pola and George Wyle.

Misery Index
    Jimmy Carter's "crisis of confidence" speech, delivered
    and televised on July 15, 1979.

Pome
"Fame," a song written by Michael Gore and Dean
Pitchford and made famous by Irene Cara in 1980.

ABOUT THE AUTHOR

Amber West is a native Californian with roots in Tennessee and Oklahoma. Her writing has appeared in journals and anthologies such as *Calyx, Rhizomes, Puppetry International, Furies: A Poetry Anthology of Women Warriors,* and *The Routledge Companion to Puppetry & Material Performance,* as well as in her chapbook entitled *Daughter Eraser.* West is creator and director of the NYC artist collective, Alphabet Arts, and the Puppets & Poets festival. Her plays and "puppet poems" have been performed on the east and west coasts. She teaches writing at the University of California, Los Angeles, and lives in Hollywood with her husband, actor Sam T. West, and their son. For updates visit amberiwest.com

ABOUT THE ARTIST

Clovis Blackwell is an interdisciplinary artist with expertise in screenprinting. His work explores themes of suffering, perseverance, and transformation, and is regularly exhibited in Southern California and internationally. He received his MFA from Azusa Pacific University in 2009 and has taught printmaking for many years. He owns and operates Fleur de Boom Editions, a publisher of limited edition fine art serigraph prints. Find out more at www.clovisblackwell.com.

OTHER WORD WORKS BOOKS

Annik Adey-Babinski, *Okay Cool No Smoking Love Pony*
Karren L. Alenier, *Wandering on the Outside*
Karren L. Alenier, ed., *Whose Woods These Are*
Karren L. Alenier & Miles David Moore, eds.,
    Winners: A Retrospective of the Washington Prize
Christopher Bursk, ed., *Cool Fire*
Barbara Goldberg, *Berta Broadfoot and Pepin the Short*
Frannie Lindsay, *If Mercy*
Elaine Magarrell, *The Madness of Chefs*
Marilyn McCabe, *Glass Factory*
Ann Pelletier, *Letter That Never*
Ayaz Pirani, *Happy You Are Here*
W.T. Pfefferle, *My Coolest Shirt*
Jacklyn Potter, Dwaine Rieves, Gary Stein, eds., *Cabin Fever:*
    Poets at Joaquin Miller's Cabin
Robert Sargent, *Aspects of a Southern Story*
    & *A Woman from Memphis*
Fritz Ward, *Tsunami Diorama*
Nancy White, ed., *Word for Word*

INTERNATIONAL EDITIONS

Kajal Ahmad (Alana Marie Levinson-LaBrosse, Mewan
    Nahro Said Sofi, and Darya Abdul-Karim Ali Najin,
    trans., with Barbara Goldberg), *Handful of Salt*
Keyne Cheshire (trans.), *Murder at Jagged Rock: A Tragedy*
    by Sophocles
Jean Cocteau (Mary-Sherman Willis, trans.), *Grace Notes*
Yoko Danno & James C. Hopkins, *The Blue Door*
Moshe Dor, Barbara Goldberg, Giora Leshem, eds.,
    The Stones Remember: Native Israeli Poets
Moshe Dor (Barbara Goldberg, trans.), *Scorched by the Sun*
Lee Sang (Myong-Hee Kim, trans.), *Crow's Eye View:*
    The Infamy of Lee Sang, Korean Poet
Vladimir Levchev (Henry Taylor, trans.), *Black Book of*
    the Endangered Species

THE WASHINGTON PRIZE

Nathalie Anderson, *Following Fred Astaire*, 1998

Michael Atkinson, *One Hundred Children Waiting for a Train*, 2001

Molly Bashaw, *The Whole Field Still Moving Inside It*, 2013

Carrie Bennett, *biography of water*, 2004

Peter Blair, *Last Heat*, 1999

John Bradley, *Love-in-Idleness: The Poetry of Roberto Zingarello*, 1995, 2nd edition 2014

Christopher Bursk, *The Way Water Rubs Stone*, 1988

Richard Carr, *Ace*, 2008

Jamison Crabtree, *Rel[AM]ent*, 2014

Jessica Cuello, *Hunt*, 2016

B. K. Fischer, *St. Rage's Vault*, 2012

Linda Lee Harper, *Toward Desire*, 1995

Ann Rae Jonas, *A Diamond Is Hard But Not Tough*, 1997

Frannie Lindsay, *Mayweed*, 2009

Richard Lyons, *Fleur Carnivore*, 2005

Elaine Magarrell, *Blameless Lives*, 1991

Fred Marchant, *Tipping Point*, 1993, 2nd edition 2013

Ron Mohring, *Survivable World*, 2003

Barbara Moore, *Farewell to the Body*, 1990

Brad Richard, *Motion Studies*, 2010

Jay Rogoff, *The Cutoff*, 1994

Prartho Sereno, *Call from Paris*, 2007, 2nd edition 2013

Enid Shomer, *Stalking the Florida Panther*, 1987

John Surowiecki, *The Hat City After Men Stopped Wearing Hats*, 2006

Miles Waggener, *Phoenix Suites*, 2002

Charlotte Warren, *Gandhi's Lap*, 2000

Mike White, *How to Make a Bird with Two Hands*, 2011

Nancy White, *Sun, Moon, Salt*, 1992, 2nd edition 2010

George Young, *Spinoza's Mouse*, 1996

THE HILARY THAM CAPITAL COLLECTION

Nathalie Anderson, *Stain*
Mel Belin, *Flesh That Was Chrysalis*
Carrie Bennett, *The Land Is a Painted Thing*
Doris Brody, *Judging the Distance*
Sarah Browning, *Whiskey in the Garden of Eden*
Grace Cavalieri, *Pinecrest Rest Haven*
Cheryl Clarke, *By My Precise Haircut*
Christopher Conlon, *Gilbert and Garbo in Love*
    & *Mary Falls: Requiem for Mrs. Surratt*
Donna Denizé, *Broken like Job*
W. Perry Epes, *Nothing Happened*
David Eye, *Seed*
Bernadette Geyer, *The Scabbard of Her Throat*
Barbara G. S. Hagerty, *Twinzilla*
James Hopkins, *Eight Pale Women*
Brandon Johnson, *Love's Skin*
Marilyn McCabe, *Perpetual Motion*
Judith McCombs, *The Habit of Fire*
James McEwen, *Snake Country*
Miles David Moore, *The Bears of Paris*
    & *Rollercoaster*
Kathi Morrison-Taylor, *By the Nest*
Tera Vale Ragan, *Reading the Ground*
Michael Shaffner, *The Good Opinion of Squirrels*
Maria Terrone, *The Bodies We Were Loaned*
Hilary Tham, *Bad Names for Women*
    & *Counting*
Barbara Louise Ungar, *Charlotte Brontë, You Ruined My Life*
    & *Immortal Medusa*
Jonathan Vaile, *Blue Cowboy*
Rosemary Winslow, *Green Bodies*
Michele Wolf, *Immersion*
Joe Zealberg, *Covalence*

THE TENTH GATE PRIZE

Jennifer Barber, *Works on Paper*, 2015
Roger Sedarat, *Haji as Puppet*, 2016
Lisa Sewell, *Impossible Object*, 2014

CPSIA information can be obtained
at www.ICGtesting.com
Printed in the USA
FSOW01n2324161117
41073FS